Editor
Eric Migliaccio

Managing Editor
Ina Massler Levin, M.A.

Editor-in-Chief
Sharon Coan, M.S. Ed.

Cover Artist
Janet Chadwick

Art Coordinator
Kevin Barnes

Art Director
CJae Froshay

Imaging
Ralph Olmedo, Jr.
Rosa C. See

Product Manager
Phil Garcia

Publishers
Rachelle Cracchiolo, M.S. Ed.
Mary Dupuy Smith, M.S. Ed.

Spelling

GRADE 1

Author

Debra J. Housel, M.S. Ed.

Teacher Created Materials, Inc.
6421 Industry Way
Westminster, CA 92683
www.teachercreated.com

ISBN-0-7439-3771-6

©2003 Teacher Created Materials, Inc.
Made in U.S.A.

Table of Contents

Introduction

The old adage "practice makes perfect" can really hold true for your child's education. The more practice and exposure your child has with concepts being taught in school, the more success he or she is likely to find. For many parents, knowing how to help their children may be frustrating because the resources may not be readily available. As a parent, it is also difficult to know where to focus your efforts so that the extra practice your child receives at home supports what he or she is learning in school.

This book has been written to help parents and teachers reinforce basic skills with children. *Practice Makes Perfect: Spelling* covers basic spelling skills for first graders. The exercises in this book can be completed in any order. The practice included in this book will meet or reinforce educational standards and objectives similar to the ones required by your state and school district for first graders:

- The student will understand consonant sounds.

- The student will recognize short vowel sounds.

- The student will know the most common digraphs' sounds and spellings.

- The student will spell high-frequency words. High-frequency words are the 1,000 words that make up 90 percent of all written material. The majority of the words presented in each spelling lesson are high-frequency words.

- The student will spell grade-level-appropriate words.

- The student will figure out how to write words based on a knowledge of word patterns (also called word families).

How to Make the Most of this Book

Here are some ideas for making the most of this book:

- Set aside a specific place in your home to work on this book. Keep it neat and tidy, with the necessary materials on hand.

- Determine a specific time of day to work on these practice pages to establish consistency. Look for times in your day or week that are less hectic and more conducive to practicing skills.

- Keep all practice sessions with your child positive and constructive. If your child becomes frustrated, don't force your child to perform. Set the book aside and try again another time.

- Review and praise the work your child has done.

- Allow the child to use whatever writing instrument he or she prefers. For example, colored pencils add variety and pleasure to drill work.

- Introduce the spelling words in the list. Discuss how the words are different and how they are alike. Read the **"In Context"** column together. Be sure that the student understands the meaning of each word.

- Assist a beginning reader in understanding directions and decoding sentences.

- Emphasize that words that end alike very often rhyme.

- If time permits, do the additional practice idea given for each lesson.

Spelling Pattern: "an"

The letters "an" form both a word and a spelling pattern. Words with the same spelling pattern often rhyme.

Words	In Context
an	I see **an** egg.
can	He **can** do it.
man	The **man** sat.
ran	I **ran** fast.
plan	We need a **plan**.
than	She did better **than** I did.
van	Do you like my new **van**?
pan	Put the ham in the **pan**.
fan	Turn off the **fan**.
began	They **began** to laugh.

Choose the word that best completes the sentence. Write it on the line.

1. The cat got into the _____. (**van, vean**)

2. A _____ came to the door. (**mann, man**)

3. Will you help me to _____ her party? (**plen, plan**)

4. The car _____ to move. (**began, begn**)

5. Clean the _____. (**pon, pan**)

6. Please turn the _____ on. (**fan, fon**)

7. He will eat _____ apple. (**an, ane**)

8. She _____ come in. (**cann, can**)

9. I want to do better _____ last time. (**than, thun**)

10. The boy _____ fast. (**ron, ran**)

- -

Cut out letters from sheets of sandpaper. (Make multiples of the most common letters: *e, a, i, o, n, s, r,* and *t*.) Have your child use the letters to form the words in the list. They need to internalize that the only difference between "pan" and "man" is the first letter.

Spelling Pattern: "an" *(cont.)*

Word Web

Write the longest word from your lesson here: _____

Write the word "an" in the center of the web below. Now write each of the remaining words from the lesson on one of the strands of the web. Here is an example:

Spelling Pattern: "at"

The letters "at" form both a word and a spelling pattern. Words with this pattern often rhyme.

Words	In Context
at	I was **at** home.
sat	He **sat** down.
cat	The **cat** ran.
rat	The **rat** ate the food.
hat	He needs a **hat**.
that	I like **that** one.
fat	Do you see the **fat** dog?
bat	She held the **bat**.
mat	Step on the **mat**.
flat	The top of the table was **flat**.

Is the **dark word** spelled wrong? If it is wrong, draw a line under it. If it is right, circle **OK**.

1. He is **at** school.   OK

2. The desk is **falt**.   OK

3. The **rat** ran away.   OK

4. Clean your feet on the **mat**.   OK

5. I want to play with the **cait**.   OK

6. She hit the ball with her **bate**.   OK

7. We **sat** at the table.   OK

8. Did Bob get **tat** book?   OK

9. She lost her **het**.   OK

10. A **fat** pig looked at me.   OK

Spray shaving cream on a desktop or on a cookie sheet. Have the child trace each spelling word in the shaving cream.

Spelling Pattern: "at" (cont.)

Rainbow Words

Which 2 words from the lesson have 4 letters? Write them here:

_____   _____

Write the rest of the words in the bands of the rainbows.   Color the rainbows.

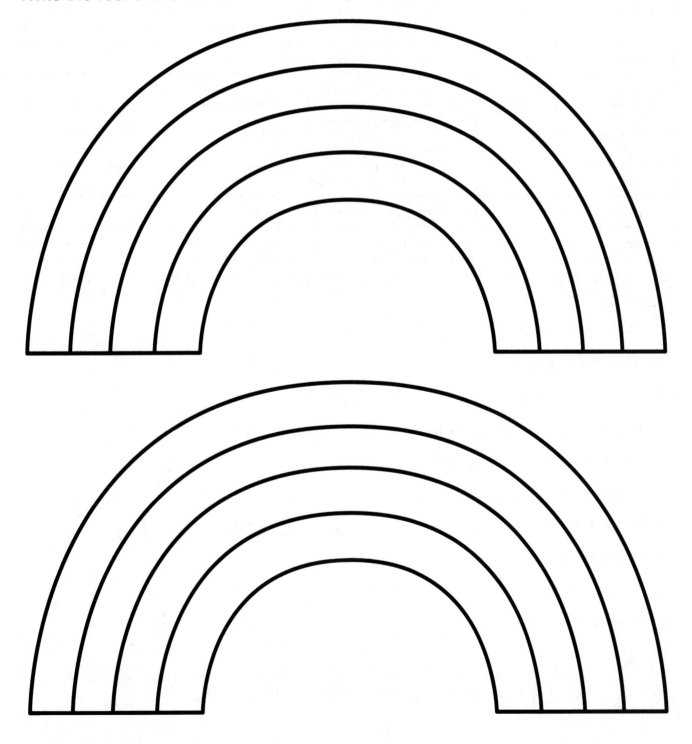

Spelling Pattern: "all"

The letters "all" form both a word and a spelling pattern. Words with this pattern often rhyme.

Words	In Context
all	The pieces were **all** there.
ball	Tim threw the **ball**.
call	Do not **call** her on the phone.
fall	Take care not to **fall** on the ice.
wall	Hang the picture on the **wall**.
tall	Liz has grown very **tall**.
hall	We came in the door and saw a long **hall**.
mall	I would like to go to the **mall**.
small	The **small** boy was lost.
squall	A **squall** is a strong storm.

Circle the word that is *not* spelled right. Write each word correctly on the line.

1. mall mal _____

2. tal tall _____

3. wlal wall _____

4. squall suqall _____

5. all al _____

6. bal ball _____

7. fall fal _____

8. kall call _____

9. smlal small _____

10. hall hal _____

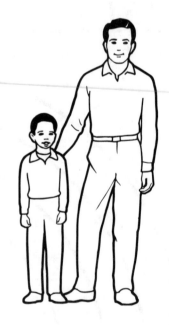

Write each spelling word once in lowercase letters and once using all uppercase letters.

Spelling Pattern: "all" (cont.)

Smiley Faces

Write the first letter of each word in the left eye. Write the last letter of each word in the right eye. Write the whole word as a smile. Here's an example:

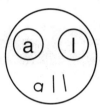

Spelling Pattern: "ack"

When the letters "ck" come together in a word, they say /k/. The letters "ack" form a spelling pattern. Words with this pattern often rhyme.

Words	In Context
back	He will be **back** in one week.
rack	Put the pan on the top **rack** of the oven.
track	She can **track** down the missing papers.
pack	They must **pack** for a trip to New York.
sack	I looked in my lunch **sack**.
lack	The ground was dry because of a **lack** of rain.
black	A panda bear is white and **black**.
shack	We looked into the **shack**.
crack	Bill saw a big **crack** in the window.
snack	Cookies make the best **snack**.

Choose the word that completes the sentence. Write it on the line.

1. The train ran off of the _____. (**trak, track**)

2. What can we eat for a _____? (**snack, snac**)

3. Put your coat on the _____. (**rak, rack**)

4. Do not use that glass! It has a _____. (**crack, crak**)

5. We went _____ to the pet shop. (**back, bak**)

6. He got a _____ dog. (**blak, black**)

7. Their home was just an old _____. (**chack, shack**)

8. I _____ the $10 I need to buy it. (**lack, lak**)

9. My dad will _____ for his trip. (**pac, pack**)

10. She put the food into a _____. (**sack, sark**)

Write each spelling word three times: once in pencil, once with colored pencil, and once with marking pen.

Spelling Pattern: "ack" *(cont.)*

Word Triangles

Write each spelling word three times to form a triangle, like this:

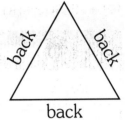

Spelling Pattern: "ed"

The letters "ed" form a spelling pattern. Words with this pattern often rhyme.

Words	In Context
bed	Please go to **bed**.
red	The flower is **red**.
fed	I **fed** the baby.
wed	The man and woman will **wed**.
led	The boy **led** the dog.
sled	She went down the hill in a **sled**.
fled	The cat **fled** from the dog.
bled	The cut on his arm **bled**.
shed	Put the tools in the **shed**.
sped	The car **sped** away.

Number the words from the list in A–Z order. You may need to look at the second letter. Then write the words in A–Z order. The first one has been done for you.

1. _____bed_____
2. _____
3. _____
4. _____
5. _____
6. _____
7. _____
8. _____
9. _____
10. _____

- -

Make some chocolate pudding (or another flavor with color) and let your child use craft sticks to "write" the words in pudding on large, sturdy pieces of heavy paper or cardboard.

Spelling Pattern: "ed" (cont.)

Word Wagons

Put the first letter in the left wheel. Put the last letter
in the right wheel. Write the whole word inside the wagon.

Spelling Pattern: "et"

The letters "et" form a spelling pattern. Words with this pattern often rhyme.

Words	In Context
get	He will **get** the book for you.
set	Please **set** the table.
let	Ron **let** the cat in.
yet	She is not here **yet**.
met	He **met** her today.
bet	I **bet** you had fun at the park.
pet	Your **pet** is cute.
wet	Do not get me **wet**!
net	Catch the fish with a **net**.
quiet	Keep **quiet**. The baby is asleep.

Is the dark word spelled wrong? If it is wrong, draw a line under it. If it is right, circle **OK**.

1. The water got me all **wet**.   OK

2. We **get** on the bus over there.   OK

3. She got the fish with a **nit**.   OK

4. My dad **met** my teacher.   OK

5. Do you have a **pet**?   OK

6. Please **ste** the dish on the table.   OK

7. Shh! Please be **quiete**.   OK

8. Will your mom **let** you come?   OK

9. I **bet** you are upset.   OK

10. He has not met my friend **tey**.   OK

- -

Write each spelling word using one color of pencil or ink for the vowels and a different color for the consonants.

Spelling Pattern: "et" *(cont.)*

Sailboats

Write each word inside the sailboat. Here is an example:

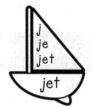

Spelling Pattern: "en"

The letters "en" form a spelling pattern. Words with this pattern often rhyme.

Words	In Context
when	Do you know **when** the bus will come?
then	I went to bed **then**.
men	Three **men** came to see me.
ten	She has **ten** cats.
open	She will **open** the box.
seven	I am **seven** years old.
women	Two **women** sat on a bench.
even	This chair is **even** bigger than the other one!
often	They went to the park **often**.
children	Six **children** played in the water.

Copy each spelling word. Count the consonants in each words. Count the vowels in each word. Fill in the numbers. The first has been done for you.

	Spelling Word	Consonants	Vowels
1.	when	3	1
2.			
3.			
4.			
5.			
6.			
7.			
8.			
9.			
10.			

11. Which word has the most consonants? _____

- -

Write each spelling word in a sentence. Use a marker to draw a box around each word from the list.

Spelling Pattern: "en" *(cont.)*

Smiley Faces

Write the first letter of each word in the left eye. Write the last letter of each word in the right eye. Write the whole word as a smile.

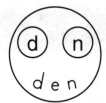

Spelling Pattern: "ell"

The letters "ell" form a spelling pattern. Words with this pattern often rhyme.

Words	In Context
fell	The child **fell** down.
bell	Please ring the **bell**.
cell	The man sat in the jail **cell**.
sell	I want to **sell** my bike.
yell	Do not **yell** at me.
well	He does not feel **well**.
tell	She can **tell** you the answer.
smell	Do you **smell** smoke?
spell	Can you **spell** big words?
shell	Pick up that sea **shell.**

Circle the word that is not spelled right. Write each word correctly on the line.

1. well wel _____

2. shell hsell _____

3. yelel yell _____

4. pells spell _____

5. smell smeel _____

6. bel bell _____

7. scell sell _____

8. tell tel _____

9. cel cell _____

10. fell fel _____

- -

Write a sentence for each spelling word. Include a plural noun (more than one person, place, or thing). Here is an example: *He fell over the logs.*

Spelling Pattern: "ell" *(cont.)*

Word Wagons

Put the first letter in the left wheel. Put the last letter
in the right wheel. Write the whole word inside the wagon.

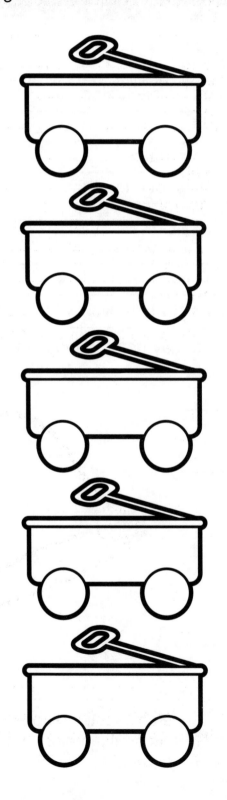

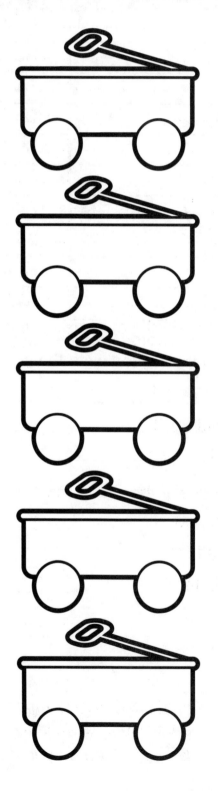

Lesson 9: "in"

Spelling Pattern: "in"

The letters "in" form both a word and a spelling pattern. Words with this pattern often rhyme.

Words	In Context
in	I got **in** the car.
win	He will **win** this game.
fin	The fish has one **fin** on each side.
pin	Do not drop that **pin**.
tin	She put the water in a **tin** cup.
thin	They need food. They look too **thin**.
skin	He had dark **skin**.
chin	She hit her **chin** on the ground.
grin	I gave them a big **grin**.
begin	We saw the truck **begin** to move.

Number the words from the list in A–Z order. You may need to look at the second letter. Then write the words in A–Z order.

1. _____

2. _____

3. _____

4. _____

5. _____

6. _____

7. _____

8. _____

9. _____

10. _____

Use each spelling word in an oral sentence or question spoken to an adult. Spell out the words in the list. Here is an example:
Begin. When do you think it will b-e-g-i-n to rain?

Spelling Pattern: "in" *(cont.)*

Word Tree

Many words "grow" from the word "in." Write "in" under the tree. Write the rest of the words from the lesson in its branches.

Spelling Pattern: "it"

The letters "it" form both a word and a spelling pattern. Words with this pattern often rhyme.

Words	In Context
it	The dog sat on **it**.
sit	May I **sit** there?
bit	The cat **bit** my hand!
hit	She will **hit** the ball with the bat.
fit	She cannot **fit** in that dress.
pit	He fell into a **pit**.
kit	We put together the toy **kit**.
quit	Don't **quit** until it is done.
unit	Our class is doing a **unit** on plants.
visit	We will **visit** your brother.

Is the dark word spelled wrong? If it is wrong, draw a line under it. If it is right, circle **OK**.

1. Please **site** down.   OK

2. We went to **visit** our aunt.   OK

3. Do not **hit** your brother!   OK

4. It is almost time to **quitt** for the day.   OK

5. Our class did a **uint** about trees.   OK

6. Ben kicked a ball. His dog ran after **it**.   OK

7. Move the table a little **bit** to the left.   OK

8. That dress does not **fitt** well.   OK

9. The bear fell into a deep **pit**.   OK

10. Can you help me to build this model car **ket**?   OK

- -

Have your child write the spelling words in alphabetical order.

Spelling Pattern: "it" *(cont.)*

Word Web

Write the longest word from your lesson here: _____

Write the word "it" in the center of the web below. Now write each of the remaining words on one of the strands of the web. Here is an example:

Spelling Pattern: "ill"

The letters "ill" form both a word and a spelling pattern. Words with this pattern often rhyme.

Words	In Context
ill	He felt **ill**.
will	I **will** help you.
still	It is **still** hot.
fill	Please **fill** my cup.
kill	She wants to **kill** the fly.
bill	They have a $10 **bill**.
hill	Can you walk up the **hill**?
pill	She took a **pill**.
spill	Do not **spill** the water.
village	We live in a little **village**.

Circle the word that is not spelled right. Write each word correctly on the line.

1. will wil _____

2. il ill _____

3. tsill still _____

4. fill fil _____

5. bil bill _____

6. pill pil _____

7. hile hill _____

8. spil spill _____

9. kill kil _____

10. vilage village _____

Ask your child to write the spelling words in sentences, allowing him or her to draw any parts of the sentence he or she chooses (except for the spelling word). Here is an example: I did not spill the ⬚SUGAR⬚.

Spelling Pattern: "ill" *(cont.)*

Word Tree

Many words "grow" from the word "ill." Write "ill" under the tree. Write the rest of the words in its branches.

Spelling pattern: "ot"

The letters "ot" form a spelling pattern. Words with this pattern often rhyme.

Words	In Context
not	The coat is **not** in there.
got	I **got** a new toy on my birthday.
lot	A **lot** of people like art.
hot	That stove is **hot**.
spot	There is a **spot** on her dress.
shot	A man **shot** at the deer.
tot	A two-year old **tot** played with the toy.
pot	Put the beans into the **pot**.
rot	Wood left outside will **rot**.
cannot	She **cannot** stop the car!

Number the words from the list in A–Z order. You may need to look at the second letter. Then write the words in A–Z order.

1. _____
2. _____
3. _____
4. _____
5. _____
6. _____
7. _____
8. _____
9. _____
10. _____

Make a chart with these headings: **Word, Vowels, Consonants.** Have the child study each word, then fill in the number of vowels and consonants in the appropriate column.

26

Spelling pattern: "ot" (cont.)

Smiley Faces

Write the first letter of each word in the left eye. Write the last letter of each word in the right eye. Write the whole word as a smile.

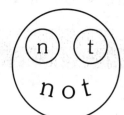

Spelling Pattern: "old"

The letters "old" form both a word and a spelling pattern. Words with this pattern often rhyme.

Words	In Context
old	The **old** man talked to us.
cold	It was **cold** outside.
hold	Will you **hold** my hand?
gold	The ring was **gold**.
told	She **told** me to stay here.
bold	The girl did not look afraid. She was **bold**.
mold	It is fun to **mold** clay.
fold	Please **fold** these shirts.
sold	He **sold** the car.
scold	My mom will **scold** me if I am late.

Circle the word that is not spelled right. Write each word correctly on the line.

1. csold scold _____

2. gold glod _____

3. sold solld _____

4. flod fold _____

5. olld old _____

6. mold modl _____

7. cold kold _____

8. told toold _____

9. blod bold _____

10. hold holed _____

- -

Allow your child to dictate a story to you, being certain to use all of the spelling words (in any order) at least once. Record the story and reread it together.

Spelling Pattern: "old" (cont.)

Word Web

Write the longest word from your lesson here: _____

Write the word "old" in the center of the web below. Write each of the other words on the remaining strands of the web. Here is an example:

Spelling Pattern: "un"

The letters "un" form a common spelling pattern. Words with this pattern often rhyme.

Words	In Context
fun	Riding a bike is great **fun**.
gun	Put down that **gun**!
run	They **run** very fast.
sun	The **sun** will set in one hour.
bun	She ate the **bun**.
nun	A **nun** went into the church.
pun	We did not understand his **pun**. (*joke*)
spun	I **spun** around to see what was behind me.
stun	This magic trick will **stun** you. (*shock; amaze*)
begun	She was late. The show had already **begun**.

Choose the word that best completes the sentence. Write it on the line.

1. The _____ began to set. (**sun, sunn**)

2. That looks like _____! (**fune, fun**)

3. I want to eat a sweet _____. (**bun, bunn**)

4. Jim will _____ around the track. (**run, rune**)

5. School has already _____. (**bgun, begun**)

6. The _____ helped the poor. (**nun, non**)

7. That ride goes so fast it will _____ you. (**tuns, stun**)

8. I did not understand her _____. (**pun, pune**)

9. He _____ around, but no one was behind him. (**psun, spun**)

10. A _____ is not a toy. (**gun, jun**)

Write each spelling word three times in a row. Circle the best handwriting for each word.

Spelling Pattern: "un" *(cont.)*

Word Triangles

Write each spelling word three times to form a triangle, like this:

Short Words Ending in "e"

Some short words end in the letter "e" and rhyme with each other.

Words	In Context
he	**He** told me a story.
she	Will **she** go on the bus?
we	Dad said that **we** have to go home.
me	Please give it to **me**.
be	It will **be** fun to play.
see	They can **see** the show.
tree	She hid high up in a **tree**.
free	This chair is **free**.
three	The little boy was **three** years old.
agree	I **agree** with you.

Is the dark word spelled wrong? If it is wrong, draw a line under it. If it is right, circle **OK**.

1. She has **thre** children.   OK

2. I think **she** is tall.   OK

3. Will you go with **mee**?   OK

4. Do you **agree** with her?   OK

5. Do you know where **hee** is?   OK

6. My class planted a **tre**.   OK

7. He will give away the candy for **free**.   OK

8. Sam should **be** in bed by that time.   OK

9. I do not **se** your glasses.   OK

10. Today **wee** played a game.   OK

- -

Work with your child to compose a rhyming poem or song using the words in the spelling list.

Short Words Ending in "e" *(cont.)*

Word Sort

Write each spelling word under the correct heading.

Has 1 Consonant

_____

_____

_____

_____

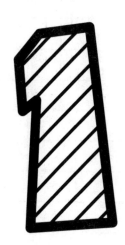

Has 2 Consonants

_____

_____

_____

_____

Has 3 Consonants

_____

_____

_____

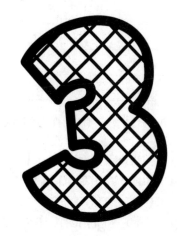

The Pair that Stays Together: "qu"

The letter "u" always follows the letter "q." Together they make the /kw/ sound.

Words	In Context
quite	It is **quite** hot in here.
quick	He always has a **quick** answer.
question	Do you have a **question**?
quilt	My mom made me a **quilt**.
quake	The pet began to **quake** from the cold.
quarter	I need a **quarter** to make a phone call.
queen	The **queen** had a gold crown.
quiz	We will have a math **quiz** next week.
equal	Each boy had an **equal** number of cookies.
square	A **square** has four equal sides.

Write each spelling word. Count the consonants in each word. Count the vowels in each word.

	Spelling Word	Consonants	Vowels
1.	_____	_____	_____
2.	_____	_____	_____
3.	_____	_____	_____
4.	_____	_____	_____
5.	_____	_____	_____
6.	_____	_____	_____
7.	_____	_____	_____
8.	_____	_____	_____
9.	_____	_____	_____
10.	_____	_____	_____

11. Which word has the most vowels? _____

Have your child dictate to you a sentence or a question for each spelling word that includes a cartoon character, fairy tale character, or super hero's name as the subject. Record the sentences, then ask the child to highlight the spelling word.

The Pair that Stays Together: "qu" *(cont.)*

Sailboats

Write each word inside the sailboat. Here is an example:

q
qu
qui
quit

Consonant Digraph: "th"

The letters "t" and "h" come together to form a digraph. The digraph makes a whole new sound.

Words	In Context
with	Come **with** me.
this	**This** is the best one?
there	You can put the desk right **there**.
other	She went to the **other** room.
mother	His **mother** is tall.
father	His **father** is short.
them	You may go with **them**.
these	Please clean **these** dirty pans.
think	I **think** that the dog is hungry.
both	My brothers **both** went to bed.

Choose the word that best completes the sentence. Write it on the line.

1. I went _____ her to the mall. **(with, wih)**

2. The bag is over _____. **(thair, there)**

3. We saw him put on the _____ coat. **(other, uther)**

4. Is _____ the first time she has been late? **(fis, this)**

5. Do you _____ that we will get there in time? **(think, thik)**

6. The boys _____ started to run. **(both, bothe)**

7. Tom ran after _____. **(tem, them)**

8. Are _____ the socks you lost? **(thees, these)**

9. Our _____ works at the bank. **(father, fater)**

10. His _____ will go to the shop. **(muther, mother)**

- -

Ask your student to write the spelling words, then underline each vowel and circle each consonant.

Consonant Digraph: "th" *(cont.)*

Word Wagons

Put the first letter in the left wheel. Put the last letter in the right wheel. Write the whole word inside the wagon.

Consonant Digraph: "ch"

The letters "c" and "h" come together to form a digraph. The digraph makes a whole new sound.

Words	In Context
each	The toys were 50 cents **each**.
reach	Can you **reach** way up there?
child	The **child** gave me a smile.
rich	That **rich** man has a lot of money.
check	Please write a **check** for $10.
church	Our school is next to a **church**.
chart	The teacher made a **chart** for the students.
which	Choose **which** shirt you want to wear.
much	I think that looks **much** better.
such	She is **such** a smart girl.

Write each spelling word. Count the consonants in each word. Count the vowels in each word. Which word has the most consonants?

	Spelling Word	Consonants	Vowels
1.	_____	_____	_____
2.	_____	_____	_____
3.	_____	_____	_____
4.	_____	_____	_____
5.	_____	_____	_____
6.	_____	_____	_____
7.	_____	_____	_____
8.	_____	_____	_____
9.	_____	_____	_____
10.	_____	_____	_____

- -

Have your child write each spelling word once in lowercase letters and once using all uppercase letters.

Consonant Digraph: "ch" *(cont.)*

Phone Code

Did you know that phones have numbers and letters on their keys? Copy each word from the list on page 38. Then write the word again using its numbers.

Spelling Word	**Phone Code for Word**
Example: couch	26824
1.	
2.	
3.	
4.	
5.	
6.	
7.	
8.	
9.	
10.	

11. What 2 letters are not on the phone keys? _____ and _____

Consonant Digraph: "sh"

The letters "s" and "h" come together to form a digraph. The digraph makes a whole new sound.

Words	In Context
should	You **should** close that door. It is cold out.
fish	She likes to catch **fish**.
ship	The **ship** set sail.
short	I am too **short** to reach it.
wish	He will **wish** for a puppy.
push	Try to **push** the door open.
wash	Please help me **wash** the car.
fresh	The oranges were **fresh**.
shop	Dad will **shop** at the store.
shoes	Where are my **shoes**?

Write each word. Does "sh" come first or last? Put an **X** in the correct box.

	Spelling Word	**"Sh" First**	**"Sh" Last**
1.	_____	☐	☐
2.	_____	☐	☐
3.	_____	☐	☐
4.	_____	☐	☐
5.	_____	☐	☐
6.	_____	☐	☐
7.	_____	☐	☐
8.	_____	☐	☐
9.	_____	☐	☐
10.	_____	☐	☐

- -

Practice Idea!

Write the spelling words using one color pencil for digraphs and another color for the rest of the word.

Consonant Digraph: "sh" *(cont.)*

Word Triangles

Write each spelling word three times to form a triangle, like this:

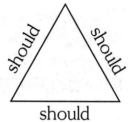

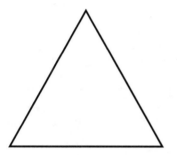 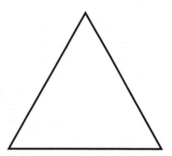 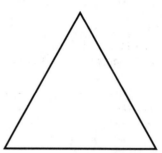

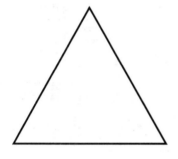 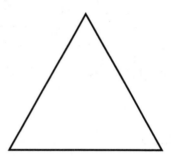 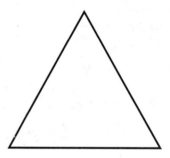

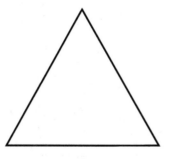 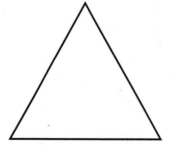

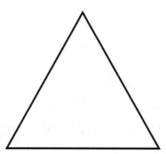 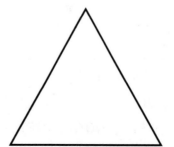

The Days of the Week

Words	In Context
Sunday	They will go to the park on **Sunday**.
Monday	School starts on **Monday**.
Tuesday	She has gym on **Tuesday**.
Wednesday	He has art on **Wednesday**.
Thursday	Our music class is on **Thursday**.
Friday	My class will go outside on **Friday**.
Saturday	We help around the house on **Saturday**.
today	Can you help me fix my bike **today**?
tomorrow	My friend will come **tomorrow**.
yesterday	It rained hard **yesterday**.

Choose the word that best completes the sentence. Write it on the line.

1. She read the paper on _____. (**Sunday**, **Sonday**)

2. He went to the bank _____. (**yestrday**, **yesterday**)

3. School opens next _____. (**Mondy**, **Monday**)

4. On _____ I like to ride my bike. (**Satruday**, **Saturday**)

5. What is the date _____? (**today**, **twoday**)

6. I will see him next _____. (**Wenesday**, **Wednesday**)

7. Do you think it will rain _____ ? (**tomorrow**, **tomorow**)

8. He had a fish fry on _____. (**Fryday**, **Friday**)

9. Let's meet on _____. (**Thursday**, **Thrusday**)

10. The test will be on _____. (**Toosday**, **Tuesday**)

- -

Ask your child to write the spelling words in sentences, allowing him or her to draw any parts of the sentence he or she chooses (except for the spelling word). Here is an example: *On Monday, I went to the* [drawing] .

The Days of the Week *(cont.)*

Label a Calendar

Fill in the days of the week across the top. Sunday has been written in for you.

Sunday						

◄ What day of the week is it today? Write **today** in the box under that day.

◄ Write **yesterday** in the box before **today**.

◄ Write **tomorrow** in the box after **today**.

Assessment #1

Read each sentence. Read all of the answers. Fill in the circle of the word that is spelled right and best completes the sentence.

1. **I ate _____ egg.**
   - (a) an
   - (b) ane
   - (c) ann

2. **He _____ ride my bike.**
   - (a) cane
   - (b) can
   - (c) cann

3. **May I see _____ book?**
   - (a) tat
   - (b) thet
   - (c) that

4. **The _____ sat on a rug.**
   - (a) cate
   - (b) cat
   - (c) cait

5. **Don't get your food on the _____!**
   - (a) wall
   - (b) whall
   - (c) wal

6. **I want to pet the _____ dog.**
   - (a) smell
   - (b) smal
   - (c) small

7. **My coat is _____.**
   - (a) bluck
   - (b) block
   - (c) black

8. **The glass had a big _____.**
   - (a) crak
   - (b) crack
   - (c) krack

9. **He just _____ those fish.**
   - (a) fed
   - (b) feed
   - (c) fede

10. **He _____ away on his bike.**
    - (a) sped
    - (b) speed
    - (c) spid

11. **Do not _____ go of the rope.**
    - (a) lot
    - (b) let's
    - (c) let

12. **Do you have a _____?**
    - (a) piet
    - (b) pet
    - (c) pete

13. **They have _____ children.**
    - (a) seven
    - (b) sevin
    - (c) sivin

14. **Three _____ were at the table.**
    - (a) wemen
    - (b) women
    - (c) wimen

15. **He will _____ the chair.**
    - (a) sell
    - (b) sel
    - (c) cell

Assessment #2

Read each sentence. Read all of the answers. Fill in the circle of the word that is spelled right and best completes the sentence.

1. **She does not feel _____.**
   ⓐ whel   ⓑ wel   ⓒ well

2. **He is not fat. He is _____.**
   ⓐ tin   ⓑ thin   ⓒ thinn

3. **When did you _____ to play the horn?**
   ⓐ begun   ⓑ began   ⓒ begin

4. **Let's go _____ my friend.**
   ⓐ visit   ⓑ vist   ⓒ viset

5. **Does the vest _____ her?**
   ⓐ fet   ⓑ fitt   ⓒ fit

6. **He will drink water to take his blue _____.**
   ⓐ pile   ⓑ pill   ⓒ pille

7. **The soup is _____ too hot to eat.**
   ⓐ stil   ⓑ still   ⓒ tsill

8. **You _____ go back there.**
   ⓐ kan not   ⓑ canot   ⓒ cannot

9. **We need a _____ of wood.**
   ⓐ lot   ⓑ lott   ⓒ lote

10. **She gave me a _____ ring.**
    ⓐ gold   ⓑ jold   ⓒ goled

11. **Your dad may _____ you.**
    ⓐ skold   ⓑ scold   ⓒ sculd

12. **The movie had already _____ when we got there.**
    ⓐ begn   ⓑ begon   ⓒ begun

13. **My mom went to the store _____.**
    ⓐ yestrday   ⓑ yesterday   ⓒ yestday

14. **They will see the doctor next _____.**
    ⓐ Wenesday   ⓑ Wednesday   ⓒ Wensday

15. **My desk is right over _____.**
    ⓐ there   ⓑ thair   ⓒ thare

Assessment #3

Read the dark word. Fill in the circle of the word that rhymes with it.

1. **rack**
   - (a) tack (b) tick (c) tock

2. **quit**
   - (a) skit (b) pet (c) treat

3. **when**
   - (a) pan (b) fin (c) men

4. **yell**
   - (a) sent (b) swell (c) belt

5. **queen**
   - (a) seen (b) dream (c) leaf

6. **them**
   - (a) lend (b) pen (c) gem

7. **reach**
   - (a) speak (b) peach (c) fish

8. **shop**
   - (a) top (b) tap (c) tip

9. **today**
   - (a) buy (b) away (c) key

10. **quake**
   - (a) beak (b) bait (c) bake

11. **should**
   - (a) would (b) wad (c) wed

12. **think**
   - (a) blank (b) block (c) blink

13. **quick**
   - (a) sick (b) sock (c) sack

14. **tree**
   - (a) fit (b) foe (c) fee

15. **mold**
   - (a) wild (b) bald (c) hold

16. **quite**
   - (a) slit (b) white (c) tint

17. **win**
   - (a) sin (b) fine (c) kind

18. **run**
   - (a) pen (b) fin (c) shun

19. **such**
   - (a) duck (b) hut (c) much

20. **short**
   - (a) cork (b) port (c) torn

Answer Key

Page 4
1. van
2. man
3. plan
4. began
5. pan
6. fan
7. an
8. can
9. than
10. ran

Page 5
longest word: began

Page 6
1. OK
2. flat
3. OK
4. OK
5. cat
6. bat
7. OK
8. that
9. hat
10. OK

Page 7
that
flat

Page 8
1. mall
2. tall
3. wall
4. squall
5. all
6. ball
7. fall
8. call
9. small
10. hall

Page 10
1. track
2. snack
3. rack
4. crack
5. back
6. black
7. shack
8. lack
9. pack
10. sack

Page 12
1. bed
2. bled
3. fed
4. fled
5. led
6. red
7. shed
8. sled
9. sped
10. wed

Page 14
1. OK
2. OK
3. net
4. OK
5. OK
6. set
7. quiet
8. OK
9. OK
10. yet

Page 16
1. when: c3, v1
2. then: c3, v1
3. men: c2, v1
4. ten: c2, v1
5. open: c2, v2

6. seven: c3, v2
7. women: c3, v2
8. even: c2, v2
9. often: c3, v2
10. children: c6, v2
11. children

Page 18
circled words
1. wel
2. hsell
3. yelel
4. pells
5. smeel
6. bel
7. scell
8. tel
9. cel
10. fel

Page 20
1. begin
2. chin
3. fin
4. grin
5. in
6. pin
7. skin
8. tin
9. thin
10. win

Page 22
1. sit
2. OK
3. OK
4. quit
5. unit
6. OK
7. OK
8. fit
9. OK
10. kit

Page 23
longest word: visit

Page 24
circled words
1. wil
2. il
3. tsill
4. fil
5. bil
6. pil
7. hile
8. spil
9. kil
10. vilage

Page 25
longest word: village

Page 26
1. cannot
2. got
3. hot
4. lot
5. not
6. pot
7. rot
8. shot
9. spot
10. tot

Page 28
circled words
1. csold
2. glod
3. solld
4. flod
5. olld
6. modl
7. kold
8. toold
9. blod
10. holed

Answer Key (cont.)

Page 30

1. sun
2. fun
3. bun
4. run
5. begun
6. nun
7. stun
8. pun
9. spun
10. gun

Page 32

1. three
2. OK
3. me
4. OK
5. he
6. tree
7. OK
8. OK
9. see
10. we

Page 33

1 Consonant

he
we
me
be
see

2 Consonants

she
tree
free
agree

3 Consonants

three

Page 34

1. quite: c2, v3
2. quick: c3, v2

3. question: c4, v4
4. quilt: c3, v2
5. quake: c2, v3
6. quarter: c4, v3
7. queen: c2, v3
8. quiz: c2, v2
9. equal: c2, v3
10. square: c3, v3
11. question

Page 36

1. with
2. there
3. other
4. this
5. think
6. both
7. them
8. these
9. father
10. mother

Page 38

1. each: c2, v2
2. reach: c3, v2
3. child: c4, v1
4. rich: c3, v1
5. check: c4, v1
6. church: c5, v1
7. chart: c4, v1
8. which: c4, v1
9. much: c3, v1
10. such: c3, v1

Page 39

1. each: 3224
2. reach: 73224
3. child: 24453
4. rich: 7424
5. check: 24325
6. church: 248724
7. chart: 24278

8. which: 94424
9. much: 6824
10. such: 7824
11. Q & Z

Page 40

1. should: first
2. fish: last
3. ship: first
4. short: first
5. wish: last
6. push: last
7. wash: last
8. fresh: last
9. shop: first
10. shoes: first

Page 42

1. Sunday
2. yesterday
3. Monday
4. Saturday
5. today
6. Wednesday
7. tomorrow
8. Friday
9. Thursday
10. Tuesday

Page 43

Answers will vary.

Page 44

1. a
2. b
3. c
4. b
5. a
6. c
7. c
8. b
9. a

10. a
11. c
12. b
13. a
14. b
15. a

Page 45

1. c
2. b
3. c
4. a
5. c
6. b
7. b
8. c
9. a
10. a
11. b
12. c
13. b
14. b
15. a

Page 46

1. a
2. a
3. c
4. b
5. a
6. c
7. b
8. a
9. b
10. c
11. a
12. c
13. a
14. c
15. c
16. b